My brother has published a volume of poetry, called *Blow Out The Candle*. The reviews were ecstatic. I hate him already.

Adrian Mole

PUBLISHED

Offally Good! – The Book! (Stoat Books, 1991)

UNPUBLISHED

Fiction:
Lo! The Flat Hills of My Homeland
Later to be retitled: *Birdwatching*

Sparg from Kronk
Or *Krog of Gork*

Sty

The Restless Tadpole

Non-fiction:
Celebrity and Madness

Plays:
The White Van

Plague!

ADRIAN MOLE
Born 2nd April 1967, Leicester

Happy 50th birthday, Adrian Mole

ADRIAN MOLE

The Collected Poems

PENGUIN BOOKS

PENGUIN BOOKS

UK | USA | Canada | Ireland | Australia
India | New Zealand | South Africa

Penguin Books is part of the Penguin Random House group of companies
whose addresses can be found at global.penguinrandomhouse.com.

First published in Great Britain by Michael Joseph 2017
001

Copyright © Lily Broadway Productions Ltd, 2017

The poems are taken from the following novels by Sue Townsend:

The Secret Diary of Adrian Mole Aged 13¾, first published by Methuen 1982
The Growing Pains of Adrian Mole, first published by Methuen 1984
The True Confessions of Adrian Albert Mole, first published by Methuen 1989
Adrian Mole: The Wilderness Years, first published by Methuen 1993
Adrian Mole: The Cappuccino Years, first published by Michael Joseph 1999
Adrian Mole and the Weapons of Mass Destruction, first published by Michael Joseph 2004
The Lost Diaries of Adrian Mole 1999–2001, first published by Michael Joseph 2008
Adrian Mole: The Prostrate Years, first published by Michael Joseph 2009

The moral right of the author has been asserted

Set in 9/2.4 pt Baskerville 10 Pro
Typeset by Jouve (UK), Milton Keynes
Printed in Great Britain by Clays Ltd, St Ives plc

A CIP catalogue record for this book is available from the British Library

ISBN: 978-0-718-18803-0

Contents

The Tap

The tap drips and keeps me awake,
In the morning there will be a lake.
For the want of a washer the carpet will spoil,
Then for another my father will toil.
My father can snuff it while he is at work.
Dad, fit a washer don't be a burk!

Untitled I

Pandora!
I adore ya.
I implore ye
Don't ignore me.

Blossoms

Little Brown Horse
Eating apples in a field,
Perhaps one day
My heart will be healed.
I stroke the places Pandora has sat
Wearing her jodphurs and riding hat.
Goodbye, brown horse.
I turn and retreat,
The rain and mud are wetting my feet.

Untitled II

PANDORA! PANDORA! PANDORA!

Oh! My love,
My heart is yearning,
My mouth is dry,
My soul is burning.
You're in Tunisia,
I am here.
Remember me and shed a tear.
Come back tanned and brown and healthy.
You're lucky that your dad is wealthy.

Untitled III

Bert, you are dead old.
Fond of Sabre, beetroot and Woodbines.
We have nothing in common,
I am fourteen and a half,
You are eighty-nine.
You smell, I don't.
Why we are friends
Is a mystery to me.

Moon's Last Quarter

The trees are stark naked.
Their autumnal clothes
Litter the pavements.
Council sweepers apply fire
Thus creating municipal pyres.
I, Adrian Mole,
Kick them
And burn my Hush Puppies.

Untitled IV

My young love,
Treacle hair and knee-socks
Give my system deep shocks
You've a magic figure:
I'm Roy Rogers, you are Trigger.

The Discontented Tuna

I am a Tuna fish,
Swimming in the sea of discontent.
Oh, when, when,
Will I find the spawning ground?

Norway

Norway! Land of difficult spelling.
Hiding your beauty behind strange vowels.
Land of long nights, short stays and dots over 'O's.
Ruminating majestic reindeers
Tread wearily on ice floes
Ever aware of what happened to the
Titanic
One day I will sojourn your shores
I live in the middle of England
But!
Norway my soul resides in your watery ~~fiords fyords~~
~~fiiords~~
Inlets.

Ode to Engels
or
Hymn to the Modern Poor

Engels, you catalogued the misfortunes of the poor in days of yore,
Little thinking that the poor would still be with us in nearly 1984.
Yet stay! What is this I see in 1983?
'Tis a queue of hungry persons outside the Job Centre.
Though rats and TB be but sad memories
The pushchairs of the modern poor contains pasty babies with hacking coughs
Young mothers draw on number six
Young fathers queue to pay fines
Old people watch life pass the plate-glass windows of council homes
Oh Engels that you were still amongst us pen in hand
Your indignation a-quiver
Your fine nose tuned to the bad smells of 1983.

Waiting for the Giro

The pantry door creaks showing empty Fablon shelves.
The freezer echoes with mournful electrical whirrings.
The boy goes ragged trousered to school.
The woman waits at the letterbox.
The bills line up behind the clock.
The dog whimpers empty-bellied in sleep.
The building society writes letters penned in vitriol.
The house waits, waits, waits,
Waits for the giro.

Mrs Thatcher

Do you weep, Mrs Thatcher, do you weep?
Do you wake, Mrs Thatcher, in your sleep?
Do you weep like a sad willow?
On your Marks and Spencer's pillow?
Are your tears molten steel?
Do you weep?
Do you wake with '*Three million*' on your brain?
Are you sorry that they'll never work again?
When you're dressing in your blue, do you see the waiting
    queue?
Do you weep, Mrs Thatcher, do you weep?

Untitled V

White face, red cheeks.
Eyes like crocus buds.
Hands deft and sure, yet worked to gnarled roots.
A practical comfortable body, dressed in young colours.
Feet twisted, and planted firmly on the ground.
A sure soft voice, with a crackly sudden laugh.
Her body is lifeless and cold.
But the memory of her is joyful and as warm as a rockpool
    in August.

The Future

What future is there for the young?
What songs are waiting to be sung?
There are no mountains left to climb,
No poetry without a rhyme.
No jobs to go to after school.
We divide and still they rule.
They give us Job Creating Schemes.
When what we want are hopes and dreams.

Daffodils

While on my settee I lie
From out of the corner of my eye
I spot a clump of Yellow Daffodils,
Bowing and shaking as a lorry goes by.
Brave green stalks supporting yellow bonnets.
Like the wife of a man who writes Love Sonnets.

Hear what he saying

Sisters and brothers listen to Jah,
Hear his words from near and far,
Haile Selassie he sit on the throne.
Hear what he saying. Hear what he saying. (*Repeated
    10 times.*)

JAH! JAH! JAH!

Rise up and follow Selassie, the king.
A new tomorrow to you he will bring. (*Repeat.*)
E-thi-o-pi-a,
He'll bring new hope to ya.
Hear what he saying. Hear what he saying. (*Repeated
    20 times.*)

Throbbing

Pandora,
I am but young
I am but small
(with cratered skin)
Yet! Hear my call.
Oh, rapturous girl
With skin sublime
Whose favourite programme's 'Question Time'
Look over here
To where I stand
A throbbing
Like a swollen gland.

Oh Hoi Polloi Reception

The food stood on the table
The drink stood on the bar
The crisps lay on the glass dish
'Twixt the gherkins in the jar.
The poets were expected
The artists had sent word
The pianists and flautists
Were bringing lemon curd.

The novelists were travelling
From dim and distant lands
The journalists were trekking
O'er deep and shifting sands
The hoi polloi stood standing
Outside the party room
Which glowed with invitation
Like a twenty-year-old womb.

Yet they dared not cross the portal
To taste the waiting feast
For fear of what would happen
If they dared to cross the beast.

The hoi polloi grew weary
And sat upon the floor
And told each other stories
Until the clock struck four.
They drew each other pictures

One person sang a song
But was careful at the end
To say 'Of course *they* won't be long.'

The artists and the poets
And the people who write books
The musicians and the journalists
And the Nouvelle Cuisine cooks
Sent word they couldn't make it
They couldn't leave the town.
They were meeting VIPs for drinks
And couldn't make it down.

The gherkins went untasted
The crisps were never crunched
The Chablis kept its cork in
The Twiglets went unmunched
But still the people waited
For a hundred million days
And just to help to pass the time
They wrote and acted plays.

They carved a pretty pattern
On the panel of the door.
They painted lovely pictures on the
Coldly concrete floor
They sang in pretty harmony
About the epic wait.
Then hush! . . . Was that a car we heard?
Was that a creaking gate?

It's the sculptors on the gravel
It's the poets wild-eyed
Quick open wide the door to
Let the journalists inside.
Oh welcome to our party!
We thought you'd never come
So sad we ate the food though
We haven't left a crumb!

For in the time of waiting
The hoi polloi grew brave
They went into the room
And took the things they craved.
And the poets and the sculptors
And the artists and the cooks
And the women good at music
And the men who wrote the books
And the journalists and actors
And the people trained to sing
Stood waiting ever after for the party to begin.

Oh Moscow Trams

Are your wheels revolutionary?
Are your carriages formed from the steel of conflict?
Are there bloodstains on the uncut moquette of
    your seats?
Do your passengers keep to the tracks of sacrifice
    and denial?
I, Adrian Mole will soon know
For in the morning I will be a fellow traveller.

Untitled VI

Sarah Ferguson, oh Sarah Ferguson,
Your name is on my lips constantly.
Don't marry Andy, his legs are bandy.
Come to Leicester, come to Leicester, marry me!
Leave the palace, grab a taxi,
I'll be waiting at the end of the M1.
We'll go to my house, meet my parents,
I know the dog and you will get along.

Nipples

Like raspberries
Taken from the freezer
Inviting tongue and lips
but warning not to bite
Not yet
soon
But not yet

On Seeing Pandora's Midriff

The glorious shoreline from ribcage
To pelvis
Like an inlet
A bay
A safe haven
I want to navigate
To explore
To take readings from the stars
To carefully trace my fingers
Along the shoreline
And eventually to guide my ship, my destroyer,
    my pleasure craft
Into and beyond your harbour

Pandora's Little Pussy

I love her little Pussy
Her coat is so warm
But if I should stroke her
She'll call the police and identify me in
A line-up
And do me some harm

Pandora! Let me!

Let me stroke your inner thighs
Let me hear your breathy sighs
Let me feel your silky skin
Let me make your senses spin
Let me touch your soft white breast
Let us stop and have a rest.
Let me join our beating hearts
Let me forge our private parts
Let me delve and make your mine
Let me give you food and wine
Let me lick you with my tongue
Let me do whatever's wrong
Let me watch you take your pleasure
Let me dress you in black leather
Let me fit you like a glove
Let me consummate our love.

Dr Braithwaite

Since you gained your Ph.D.
You've had no time for me.
You loved me once, you could again.
Pandora, give up other men!
You swore to love me for all time.
As long as Moon and June would rhyme.
Please marry me and be my wife.
For you I'll sacrifice my life.
I'll stay at home, I'll cook and clean
In the background, never seen.
When you return from brainy toil,
I'll have the kettle on the boil.
While you translate from Serbo-Croat,
I will shake our coco doormat.
I'll gladly wash your duvet cover,
If only I can be your lover.

Untitled VII

Gentle face,
Night black hair,
Natural Grace,
Love I swear.
Marry me, be my wife,
Make me happy, share my life.

Untitled VIII

Oh Greece, ancient cultured land
You wrap around my heart just like
An old elastic band.
Your hag-like women pensioners
Clad in clothes of black,
Are they unaware of all the services they lack?
Will they be content to watch
The donkey with its load?
Won't they want a vehicle to
Drive along the road?

Oh Diana!

Oh Diana! Was a song, of
my mother's youth. Sung by
Paul Anka, who was small
and white of tooth.
The refrain, *Oh Diana!*
Beats inside Mum's head.
A blank, a blank, a doo-dah
that her Diana is dead.

Glen Bott

Seen from a distance
Tall, frowning, twelve.
Gangsta clothes
In an English market.
Half of Sharon, half of me.
Fully himself.

Untitled IX

Mystery Guest
That's the test
Play the game
If you know the name.

Requiem for Mrs Wormington

She was not a little old lady
She was six foot tall.
She didn't smile sweetly
She wouldn't play ball.
She didn't wear chiffon
Or white gloves to wave.
She lived through two wars
But wasn't called brave.
She drew her own curtains
And cooked her own dinners
She worked in a factory with good folk and sinners.
Her overdraft didn't exceed £1.50.
But she didn't get praised for being so thrifty.
Farewell, Mrs Wormington, fan of Nye Bevan
I hope you are warm again up there in heaven.

Poem to Dave

Dave Mutter, Dave Mutter
His name is so charming.
My passion for him though
Is slightly alarming.
For 55 minutes
Two sessions a week
I sit on his sofa
In anguish and speak
Of my heartache and longing
And alienation
From family and friends
And the rest of the nation.

Untitled X

Mr Blair,
You have nice hair.
You blink a lot
To show you care.
Dictators quail
And tyrants wince,
Prime Minister,
You are a prince.

Daisy

It's not your eyes I miss,
It's not your hair.
Your lips I'd like to kiss,
But you're not there.
It's not your skin I need,
It's not your face.
With every book I read,
I feel your grace.
I scan a newspaper,
I watch TV.
But see nothing there,
Return to me.

I'll burn my cardigans,
Update my glasses.
Eat crisps another way,
I'll join the masses.
Learn to rock 'n' roll,
Watch *EastEnders*.
Like R & B and soul,
And gender benders.
I'll watch *Big Brother* live,
And the repeat.
I'll educate myself
By reading *Heat*.

I will embrace *The Wire*
And ditch my *Newsnight*.
Oh, Daisy, light my fire,
And soothe my Dark Knight.

To My Organ

Oh staunched rod of old,
Why art though now so limp and cold?
Has desire fled from thee?
Art though anxious to be free
Of love's quick flame so
Quickly quenched?
Will you lift your head again?
And if 'yes' please, rod, tell me when.

'I ruthlessly exploited Adrian. But he can't afford to sue me.'
Sue Townsend

The John Tydeman Letters

Dear Adrian Mole,

Thank you for the poems which you sent to the BBC and which somehow landed up on my desk. I read them with interest and, taking into account your tender years, I must confess that they do show some promise. However, they are not of sufficient quality for us to consider including them in any of our current poetry programmes. Have you thought of offering them to your School Magazine or to your local Parish Magazine? (If you have one.)

If, in future, you wish to submit any of your work to the BBC may I suggest you get it typed out and retain, also, a copy for yourself. The BBC does not normally consider submissions in handwritten manuscript form and, despite the neatness of presentation, I did have some difficulty in making out *all* of the words – particularly at the end of one poem entitled 'The Tap' where there was a rather nasty blotch which had caused the ink to run. (A teastain or a tear-stain? A case of 'Your Tap runneth over'!)

Since you wish to follow a literary career I suggest you will need to develop a thick skin in order to accept many of the inevitable future rejections you may receive with good grace and the minimum of personal pain.

With my best wishes to you for future literary efforts – and, above all, Good Luck!

Yours sincerely,
John Tydeman

P.S. I enclose a poem by a certain John Mole which appeared in this week's *Times Literary Supplement*. Is he a relation? It is very good.

Dear Adrian Mole,

Thank you for submitting your latest poem. I understood it perfectly well once it had been typed. However, Adrian, understanding is not all. Our Poetry Department is inundated with autumnal poems. The smell of bonfires and the crackling of leaves pervade the very corridors. Good try, but try again, eh?

Yours with best wishes,
John Tydeman

British Broadcasting Corporation
19th July

Dear Adrian Mole,

Thank you for your very neat letter and for the new poem entitled 'Norway'. It is a considerable development on your previous work and indicates that you are maturing as a poet. If your School Magazine rejected 'Norway' then the Editor of the magazine probably needs his (or her) head seeing to. Unless, of course, you have a lot of very good poets at your school. I agree with you about those boring rhyming poems about flowers and stuff but you must remember that before you can break the rules of rhyme and rhythm you do have to know what those rules are about. It is like a painter who wishes to do abstract paintings – he has to know how to draw precisely from life before he jumbles things up. Picasso is a very good case in point to cite.

I hope you were successful in your test on the Norwegian Leather Industry. The Norwegian colleague (he is a Radio Producer in Bergen, Norway) to whom I showed your poem was very impressed that you were studying his country so diligently. I attach a translation of a letter he sent you which must have been rather difficult to understand since it was in Norwegian. Incidentally, I think 'Fjords' is a better word than 'Inlets'. Don't worry about the spelling, a good editor will always correct details like that. I like your use of the explosive 'But!' in the penultimate line. There isn't anything practical I can do with this particular work but I will put it on the file as an *aide memoire* to your progress as a poet (remember there is not much money in poetry . . .).

I seldom get to see Terry Wogan in the corridors as he works in Radio Two and I work for Radios Three and Four. Also his show goes on the air very early and he has usually left the building by the time I get to my desk.

With my best wishes and again my thanks for having let me see your latest work.

Yours sincerely,
John Tydeman (Radio Four)

British Broadcasting Corporation
17th September

Dear Adrian Mole,

Thank you for your latest letter (undated – you must, if you are going to be a writer – and even if you are not – date your letters. We file them, you know. The BBC has lots of files, some of which are kept in warehouses in Ware, Herts, others of which are at Caversham, nr Reading. Some of the files are very valuable.)

The country seems to have made you gloomy. It often makes poets gloomy, people like Wordsworth & Co. On other occasions it uplifts them – skylarks singing, lambs bounding, daffodils daffing, waterfalls crashing. It provokes odes and things in them. So forget gloom and suicide and write something cheerful.

I'm afraid that the poem is not yet up to broadcast standard but it does show a poetic advance, so keep on trying. We will naturally respect your copyright in your work. (The BBC is usually very good about things like that.) Copyright is dealt with by a special department and we do not bother the Director General directly with such matters. However, you have not got your break (chance) – yet.

Do not kill yourself because of another rejection. If all poets killed themselves because of early rejections there would be no poetry at all.

Yours most sincerely,
John Tydeman

British Broadcasting Corporation
30th May

Dear Adrian Mole,

I do not think I will call you 'Aidy' and I think that it is a little premature in our correspondence for you to call me 'Johnny'. In fact I am never known as 'Johnny', only as 'John'. I do not wish to sound like a stuffy old grown-up, but when you are writing to people officially it is polite for someone of your years to address them formally – though I do not mind, at this stage in our correspondence, your addressing me as 'Dear John Tydeman'. But 'Johnny', no! I do have several nicknames by which my friends know me but I am not going to reveal them to you. They relate largely to my surname rather than my Christian name.

Your last letter was altogether rather peculiar. Had you been at your parents' cocktail cabinet by any chance? Or had you drained the dregs of the previous night's vino? I do hope you had not tried glue-sniffing again. At least I am very pleased to hear that you have decided not to kill yourself this year. It would be a shocking waste. A poet can only die young when he has written a number of successful poems – *vide*: Keats, Shelley, Chatterton and Co. Most poets write drivel in their old age – *vide*: Wordsworth and quite a lot of Tennyson. I am sure your mother would miss you very much, so it is best that you remain alive.

Perhaps under the influence of something or other, your grammar seems to have gone to pot, e.g.: 'I have wrote some.'

But your poem 'Autumn Renewal' certainly has its moments.
I like the pun about chaps. A bit rude though. 'Dandeline'
(sic – not 'sick'!) is actually spelt 'dandelion' so you can't
make it rhyme with 'decline' nor 'Vaseline' – try as you will.

Do not worry about our files. They will be shredded before
the KGB can get to them. Your secrets are safe in Ware and
Caversham.

With my best wishes and continued good luck with your
writing efforts.

Yours,
John Tydeman

Dear Adrian,

To be perfectly honest, Adrian, my heart sank when I returned from holiday and saw that your manuscript, *Lo! The Flat Hills of My Homeland* had landed on my desk yet again. You say in your letter, 'I expect you are busy'. Yes, I damned well *am* busy, incredibly so.

What exactly is a 'coffee break'? I've never had a 'coffee break' during the whole of my long career with the BBC. I drink coffee at my desk. I do not go to a 'coffee break' lounge where I loll about on a sofa and read handwritten manuscripts, 473 pages long. My advice to you (without reading your wretched MS) is to:

1) Learn to type

2) Cut it by at least half

3) Supply a SAE and postage. The BBC is suffering from a cash crisis. It certainly cannot afford to subsidize your literary outpourings.

4) Find yourself a *publisher*. I am *not* a publisher. I am the Head of Radio Drama. Though sometimes I wonder if I am Marjorie Proops.

I am sorry to have to write to you in such terms, but in my experience it is best to be frank with young writers.

Yours, with best wishes,
John Tydeman

Dear Adrian,

When my secretary handed me your letter and your manuscript of *Lo! The Flat Hills of My Homeland* yet again, I thought I must be hallucinating.

You have more cheek than a Samurai wrestler, more neck than a giraffe. The BBC does not run a free photocopying service. As to your laughable suggestion that your novel be read as one of our classic serials . . . The writers of such texts are usually dead, their work having outlived them. I doubt if your work will outlive you. I am returning the manuscript immediately. Owing to an administrative error, a photocopy *was* taken. I am sending this on to you, though with great reluctance. You really must not bother me again.

John Tydeman

Sue Townsend was born in Leicester in 1946. Despite not learning to read until the age of eight, leaving school at fifteen with no qualifications and having three children by the time she was in her mid-twenties, she always found time to read widely. She also wrote secretly for twenty years. After joining a writer's group at The Phoenix Theatre Leicester, she won a Thames Television award for her first play, *Womberang*, and became a professional playwright and novelist. After the publication of *The Secret Diary of Adrian Mole Aged 13¾,* Sue continued to make the nation laugh and prick its conscience. She wrote seven further volumes of Adrian's diaries and five other popular novels – including *The Queen and I* and *Number Ten* – and numerous well-received plays. Sue passed away in 2014 at the age of sixty-eight. She remains widely regarded as Britain's favourite comic writer.

The bestselling diaries of
Adrian Mole

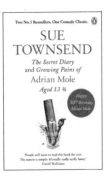

Two No.1 Bestsellers. One Comedy Classic.

SUE TOWNSEND
The Secret Diary
and *Growing Pains of*
Adrian Mole
Aged 13 ¾

'People will want to read this book for ever.
The reason is simple: it's really really really funny'
David Walliams

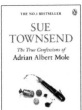

THE NO.1 BESTSELLER

SUE TOWNSEND
The True Confessions of
Adrian Albert Mole

'Wonderfully funny and sharp as knives'
Sunday Times

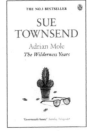

THE NO.1 BESTSELLER

SUE TOWNSEND
Adrian Mole
The Wilderness Years

'Enormously funny' *Sunday Telegraph*

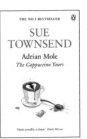

THE NO.1 BESTSELLER

SUE TOWNSEND
Adrian Mole
The Cappuccino Years

'Quite possibly a classic' *Daily Mirror*

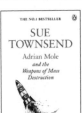

THE NO.1 BESTSELLER

SUE TOWNSEND
Adrian Mole
*and the
Weapons of Mass
Destruction*

'The funniest book of the year. I can think of
no more comical read' *Jeremy Paxman*

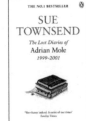

THE NO.1 BESTSELLER

SUE TOWNSEND
The Lost Diaries of
Adrian Mole
1999–2001

'Very funny indeed. A satire of our times'
Sunday Times

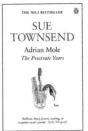

THE NO.1 BESTSELLER

SUE TOWNSEND
Adrian Mole
The Prostrate Years

'Brilliant, sharp, honest, moving, so
exquisite social comedy' *Daily Telegraph*